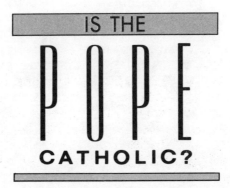

IS THE

POPE

CATHOLIC?

To Eric Newton,
a great insomniac and editor

Illustrations by Ed Powers

©1988 by Mary Ann Hogan, Lynda Seaver and Kathleen S. Lowenthal
Illustrations ©1988 by Price Stern Sloan, Inc.
Published by Price Stern Sloan, Inc.
360 North La Cienega Boulevard, Los Angeles, California 90048

ISBN 0-8431-1858-X

IS THE

P O P E

CATHOLIC?

and other amazing papal facts

by Mary Ann Hogan,
Kathleen S. Lowenthal and
Lynda Seaver

PRICE STERN SLOAN
Los Angeles

ntroduction

Does the Pope get frequent flier points? Does he carry a business card? Does the Pope party or shoot hoops? What do you have to do to become Pope, and what do you do if you decide, after a few months, that you just aren't cut out for the job?

Here is everything you've always wanted to know about the Pope but were afraid to ask, either because,

A) You are a Catholic and afraid of being excommunicated, or,

B) you are afraid of turning into a Catholic.

We have compiled this list to show that, despite his titles and fancy hats, the Pope (the current one as well as his 263 predecessors) is just like you and me–a regular guy who puts on his cassock one sleeve at a time.

 Is the Pope Catholic?

 Does a bear sleep in a cave? Not always, actually. Sometimes Popes are Jewish, though this hasn't happened in a long time. Pope Clement, who lived from 88 to 97 A.D., was the last Jewish Pope. He converted after ascending the throne. The first was St. Peter, who was also the first Pope. Catholicism, as a word, wasn't really used until the 4th Century. So the entire motley crew of Popes from the first three centuries technically were not Catholic.

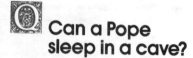

Q Can a Pope sleep in a cave?

A Is a bear Catholic? The story goes that in the year of our Lord 1294, there was a bitter struggle for the papal throne. Tired of the preceeding two-year vacancy, a religious letter-writer sent a missive to Rome: quit dilly-dallying and pick a Pope. In July, as a joke, the powers that be named him—a longtime monk who had been living in a cave—as their man. But the joke was on them. Pope Celestine V couldn't stand the pressure, and was back in his cave by winter.

Does the Pope have a blender?

No. But you can send him one. Address all gifts to: His Holiness, The Pope, Vatican City, Europe. That's it; there's no PO box, no zip code—just like Santa Claus.

Do not bother sending Sony Walkmans or Reebok athletic shoes, favorites among the thousands of gifts received by the Pope each year. If your gift is art or ceramics (ceramics are a "big" item, the Vatican says), it goes to the Vatican museum. If it is food, clothing, Walkmans or the like, it gets distributed to the needy. Don't expect a personal "thank you." The Secretary of State of the Vatican will write you instead.

Does the Pope work out?

 John Paul II certainly has what it takes to be a poster Pope. An avid skier, walker and swimmer, he had a 25-meter pool installed at the papal summer home in Castel Gandolfo. But just why he doesn't favor the bowling alley installed by Pope John XXIII (1958-63) is anybody's guess.

Q Was Pope Innocent innocent?

A Which one? There were 13 (XIII, as the Romans say). Some Innocents were, some weren't. Most of them were known for their good works. Number XII (1691-1700) abolished nepotism in the late 17th Century; number VIII (1484-92) was called "honest" for publicly acknowledging his many illegitimate children.

As for whether Pope Pius was pious: Two were saints, V (1566-1572) and XII (1939-1958), and one, Pius II (1458-64) had an early reputation as a bisexual philanderer before he cleaned up his act on the way up to the throne.

Does the Pope get "frequent flier" points?

There is no Pope Air, so JPII, the most traveled Pope, goes commercial. There's no reason he can't be a "frequent flier" provided he flies the same airline. Trouble is, whoever happens to host his visit chooses the carrier. So it could be Alitalia or Air Ozark.

Friendly skies footnote: Pope Urban VIII (1623-44) once allowed one Friar Joseph of Copertino to kiss his holy feet. Joseph was so ecstatic that he levitated in an other-worldly trance. The Pope may have been impressed. On a later day, Joe became a saint–the patron saint of air travel.

Where do old Johns go?

There have been more Pope Johns than any other, 22 in number, though our last John took the number XXIII when he ascended the throne in 1958. The fact that there have been so many just may account for this rogue's gallery of fatal footnotes. To wit:

John VIII was killed by relatives in 882. John XI was deposed, and died in prison in 935. In 964, John XII was beaten to death by the husband of his mistress after having been scorned during his lifetime for his bad grammar. John XIV was imprisoned in 984, and starved to death. John XX never died, because he never existed. They skipped over him to correct a numerical error dating back to the 10th Century, when someone counted two Johns for the price of one. John XXI was killed in 1277 when the ceiling fell in on him. He was sleeping at the time.

Nearly 700 years would pass before another Pope picked that name.

Which came first, the Pope or the egg?

The Pope, who then named the egg. Eggs Benedict, brunch of stars and saints alike, was the name given a favorite Vatican dish of Pope Benedict XIII. Pius XI (1922-39) favored a supper of hardboiled eggs, bread and wine (no wonder he ate alone). John Paul II likes his eggs with his breakfast of holy champions—ham, bacon, oatmeal, coffee and juice. Pius V (1566-72) was, no doubt, fond of eggs, though his culinary favorite was quince tart, a recipe he included in the first papal cookbook, "The Cooking Secrets of Pope Pius V." Honest to God.

Does the Pope read romance novels?

Barbara Cartland is not on the Pope's best-seller list. In fact, up until 21 years ago, you probably wouldn't have caught him reading Balzac, either. In 1966 the Church finally ended the "Librorum Prohibitorum," a list of books banned to Catholics because of their prurient or otherwise unholy contents. The ban of questionable books had survived 400 years. It was instituted by Pope Paul IV (1555-59), the same fellow who wanted to paint pants on the naked figures in the Sistine Chapel.

Does the Pope watch TV?

Well, he may not keep up with "L.A. Law" or "Dallas," but JPII likes the nightly newscasts. He recently installed cable and satellites, but the Pope doesn't watch MTV. He has PTV. These days, JPII is giving us that high-tech religion with the addition of his own video. A collection from his homily hit parade, the video sells for $29.95. Beta or VHS.

Q Does the Pope read the comics?

A If the Pope wants to peruse the Sunday funnies, he'll have to subscribe to another paper. His own Vatican fish-wrapper, "L'Osservatore Romano," is a daily diary of papal productivity. No want ads, no Macy's pullouts, no advice columns, not even a horoscope. Just all the news that's fit to Pope.

Q Is the cantaloupe a fruit or a vegetable?

A Neither. It's a former papal estate near Rome. Actually called Cantelupo, the town is where the Armenian melon was first cultivated. The cantaloupe is the fruit of the Popes. Good with Eggs Benedict, too.

Does the Pope carry a business card?

If he does, it's pretty big. His full title reads:
His Holiness the Pope
Bishop of Rome and Vicar of Jesus Christ,
Successor of St. Peter, Prince of the Apostles,
Supreme Pontiff of the Universal Church.
Patriarch of the West, Primate of Italy.
Archbishop and Metropolitan of the Roman Province, Sovereign of Vatican City.
John Paul II

(Maybe that's why he doesn't need a zip code.)

Q Does the Pope carry a driver's license?

 A JPII never left home without it during his days as a priest and bishop in Poland. But his Cardinal rule was "leave the driving to the chauffeur." This so he could catch up on papal work in the back seat. These days the task of driving the Popemobile—the bullet-proof chariot of choice —falls on a church deacon.

But Pius XI (1922-39) kept a fleet of 16 cars, three of them convertibles, in the Vatican garage. Pius XII (1939-58) was the papal speed demon, who would clock his chauffeur on the 17.4-mile road to his summer home, Castel Gandolfo, chiding him if he took more than 18 minutes. Holiness in the fast lane.

Can the Pope take a vacation?

As often as he wants. JPII likes an occasional canoe trip down some lazy river. When roughing it, the Pope likes to take a portable altar for vacation Mass, and he's been known to fashion his cross out of canoe paddles.

Stranger papal outings were recorded by World War II Popes Pius XI and XII who were known to beat a hasty vacation retreat whenever Hitler came to call. They further infuriated the Fuhrer by closing the Sistine Chapel indefinitely for repairs.

Where do Popes come from?

 Certainly not from the Holy Cabbage Patch. Most came from Rome and other parts of Italy. In fact, JPII was the first non-Italian in 455 years. Other Popes came from Greece, Spain, England, France and Africa.

Has there ever been a Pope of color?

 We don't know because we don't have the snapshots. But the three African Popes, from the northern part of the continent, were called "dark-skinned," "well-tanned," or Mediterranean. The first Pope, Peter, remember, was from the Middle East.

Does the Pope party?

Undoubtedly the biggest party animal was Leo X (1513-21), known as a hedonist, frequenter of balls, banquets, musical parties, bullfights, you name it. A great amasser of wealth and enjoyer of earthly delights, Leo is famous for his line, "Let us enjoy being Pope since God has made us one." He may have been the bad example that drove Paul IV (1555-1559), a few years later, to try for the Sistine Chapel bloomer paint job.

Pius XII was fond of an occasional nip, saying that the fruit of the vine was good for digestion and all-around health. He was known to pass the flask, even though he cautioned against excess.

Leo XIII kept a flask of a popular 19th Century cocaine-based elixir on hand.

The papal party pooper had to have been Pius V. When he wasn't eating quinces, he was imposing strict edicts to curb parties, banquets, weddings—even fancy dress and tavern-hopping. Perhaps he took the Reformation too seriously.

Why has there never been a Pope Bruce?

Bruce just wasn't one of those lucky names. The tradition of Popes renaming themselves when taking the throne began with Mercury (533-535), too fast and loose a name for your basic Roman Catholic leader. When Poped, Mercury took the name of John II, after the first, a martyr. Later, a Peter, Bishop of Pavia, took the name of John (983-84), as well, because, as we all know, only St. Peter of apostle fame could be a Peter. He was the 14th in the aforementioned long line of Johns. Footnote: only 32 names have been used by 144 Popes since the 11th Century. Note that while John, Benedict, Clement, Gregory, Innocent and Pius have rated more than 10 Popes each, there has been only one Pope Fabian (236-50) and only one Eusebius.

Q How many Popes can you fit into a century?

A Pope-stuffing was a popular sport between 867 and 965. In all, there were 28 Popes then, roughly equal to the number of college students who can cram into a phone booth.

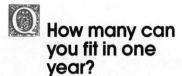 **How many can you fit in one year?**

The limit, it seems, is three. In 1045, Sylvester III, Clement II and Benedict IX handed the Popely duties down the line. Innocent V, Adrian V and John XXI shared the spotlight in 1276. In 1978, Paul VI, John Paul I and the current Pope came 1-2-3 between June and October.

 Was there ever a woman Pope?

It depends on who you ask. Papal legend has a Joan cropping up somewhere in the 9th or 10th Century. Joan fell for a monk and apparently dressed in drag to conceal her identity. A skilled papaltician, she eventually became Pope, but her identity was discovered on the way to her papal consecration, when she gave birth. She was dragged away immediately and stoned to death.

The Joan legend goes a step further. Perpetrators of the story passed on the tale of a commode-like chair, used first by Boniface VIII (1294-1303), on which prospective Popes were to sit. A deacon was dispatched to peak under the holy robes, announcing "Habet" (he has them) if the Pope passed the test.

Can a Pope sell out?

 Benedict IX (1032-48) did, for 1,500 pounds, a lot of money a millennium ago. Bennie sold his papacy to his own godfather in order to pursue marriage. The marriage didn't pan out; neither did the godfather. Godfather Gregory VI's reign lasted from May 1045 to December 1046. As for Benedict, job placement outside the papacy proved too tough. He returned to the throne in 1047. He ended up as Pope three times in 16 years. Just couldn't hold a job.

 Can the Pope pull a rabbit out of his hat?

A There were at least two so-called magician Popes: Sylvester I (314-350) and Sylvester II (999-1003). Sly I supposedly cured Emperor Constantine of leprosy and quelled a dragon who loved to dine on human flesh. Sly II was a skilled chemist and astronomer. His enemies, fearing what they perceived to be "magical powers," left him alone.

Closer to home, rumors spread about the miracles of Pius X (1903-14) after two sisters were cured of disease, and a child cured of her crippled foot after donning one of his socks. The Pope lamented, "Now they are saying...that I have started working miracles. As if I didn't have enough to do already."

Who were the great Popes and why?

You may have your favorites, as we have ours. But there were really only three Popes called "great:"

St. Leo the Great (440-61), must have been a great persuader. He talked Attila the Hun out of invading Rome.

St. Gregory the Great (590-604), managed great things for someone who was initially so scared by his election to Popehood that he hid out in a wicker basket. He hid out for three days before submitting. Gregory (of chant fame) was known, among other things, as a great punster.

St. Nicholas the Great (858-867). If you're thinking Santa Claus, forget it. Santa was fashioned after a 4th-century bishop whose bones were later stolen. As for Pope Nicholas, nobody seems to know what his story was. The Unknown Pope.

What does the Pope keep in his pockets?

A lot of things, and nothing. Leo XIII (1878-1903) stuffed a red skullcap that he should have given to the fellow who dresses him upon election, and who immediately becomes a Cardinal. But Leo, occasionally absent-minded, managed to obliterate years of papal tradition at the drop of a hat. A few weeks later he corrected his error and crowned the new Cardinal.

Pius XII (1939-1958), on the other hand, kept absolutely nothing in his pockets, to the dismay of a mugger who tried to rob him. Said the Pope to the culprit: "I have neither money nor food. I have given it to the poor of the city."

Can you engage the Pope in small talk?

Sure, after you've done the regular protocol of kneeling and kissing his ring. If he's interested or up to it, his face will show it, according to Vatican insiders. JPII loves to talk about skiing and he's been known to tell a joke or two. So if he looks relaxed, feel free to break out the knock-knocks. But remember—he only speaks English, Italian, Latin, Polish, French, German, Spanish and a smattering of Japanese, Tagalog and various African dialects.

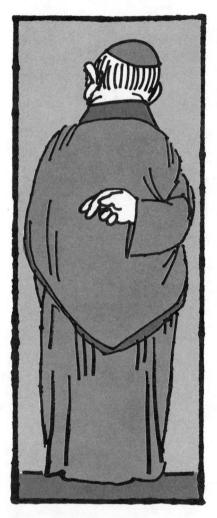

 Can the Pope tell a lie?

Does a chicken have lips? According to the so-called Doctrine of Infallibility, the Pope can only tell the truth, the whole truth and nothing but the truth in matters of faith and morals to be held by the Universal Church. The doctrine, created by Pius IX (1846-78), often is misunderstood. It doesn't necessarily mean the Pope is infallible in every other way. He can unwittingly give you wrong directions to the Vatican bowling alley. As one papal historian describes it, "(the doctrine) does not mean that the Pope can't tell an infallible joke or sneeze infallibly."

Can you call a Pope by his nickname?

The usual address is "Your Holiness." But intimates have been known to get cozier. Pope Sergius IV (1009-12) was known as "pig mouth" in his early days. Karol Wojtyla, J2P2 to San Francisco comics, still is called "Lolek," his childhood name, by friends. John XXIII (1958-1963) was known around the grounds as "Johnnie Walker" because of his fondness for taking off, unannounced, on walks, irritating the security forces. And Urban VI (1378-89), known as "the little Bishop," had a nickname for his own nephew Francesco Prignano: "Fatty."

Would the Pope walk a mile for a Camel?

 John XXIII (1958-63), aka Johnnie Walker, would. He was an avid smoker as well as a stroller. There was a onetime cheroot smoker as well, Pius XI (1922-1939), who gave up the noisome open-ended cigars for the Popehood—and at least one snuff sniffer, Pius XII (1939-58), who gave it up after a bout with pneumonia.

What is the Holy See?

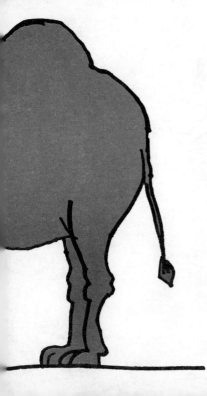 Not to be confused with the Holy Do, the See is the administrative government of the Vatican. Its top dog, JPII, is followed by Secretary of State and several advisers. The Holy See used to reach high C with the help of "castrati," boys who were bereft of their would-be manhood for the sake of preserving their high voices. The law on castrati changed under Pope Clement XIV (1769-79), who decreed that those who performed castrations would be excommunicated. Even so, the boys who had undergone the knife were still welcomed to sing in the Vatican choir.

Is the Pope a good sport?

Any number were. Pius XII (1939-1958) said sport was a way of bringing men closer to God, though like wine, it shouldn't be enjoyed to excess. In a famous story, the Harlem Globetrotters visited the Pope, produced a basketball and proceeded to practice circle-passing with Pius in the middle, merrily tapping his feet as the athletes whistled "Sweet Georgia Brown." It was Pius as well who allowed the Swiss Guard, keepers of the Vatican gate, to have their own football team.

Who can take the Swiss Guard seriously?

The Swiss Guard exists for the sole purpose of guarding the Vatican. They are mostly ceremonial, and tourists have been known to laugh themselves silly at their blue and gold, pointy-toed Renaissance garb. But don't let the court-jester look fool you. Should the occasion arise, the Guard is just as swift and sure as any top-notch security force. During World War II, Pius XII armed the guards with machine guns to protect the Vatican from the Fascists. And they must be doing their job. When did anyone take the Vatican by storm?

 Who was the longest-reigning Pope?

The longest was Pius IX (1846-1878), our man in the Vatican for 32 years, starting in 1846, father of the First Vatican Council and the famous Doctrine of Infallibility (see: "Can the Pope tell a lie?").

The shortest reign would have to go to Stephen II, elected in March 375. He died three days later, before the ceremony.

Why did the Pope cross the road?

To get to the other side, of course, but just what he found there is what really concerns us.

St. Peter, for example, headed down the Appian Way to flee the tyranny of Rome when he saw an apparition of Jesus on the other side, asking, "Quo vadis?" (Where are you going?) Feeling guilty for giving up so soon, Peter went back to Rome. He was crucified.

During World War II, Pius XII crossed the road several times to tend to those who had been injured during German air raids and the bombing of the Vatican.

As a boy, JPII should have crossed the road a little sooner to avoid being hit by a truck. He suffered a fractured skull and lay in the road until the next morning.

STOP
FOR
POPES
AND
CHICKS

Q Does the Pope wear pajamas?

A Only his most inner circle knows for sure what he wears to bed. His everyday rompers are white cassocks, floor-length robes. When he celebrates Mass he dresses no differently than other priests, with a cassock, a tunic-like alb and a chasuble, which resembles a poncho. The cone-shaped hat is a miter, the traditional bishop's hat. His walking staff is a crozier.

Why does he wear the red cape when he goes glad-handing? To keep warm.

What does he wear under his cassock? Boxer shorts, but probably not decorated. Anybody's guess. No one will say for sure.

Does the Pope have a fan club?

 The Italian tourist industry thinks so. JPII was awarded the gold medal of the Colosseum for attracting more than 5 million tourists in the first six months of his reign.

Does the Pope get mad money?

The Pope doesn't get an allowance, but the Holy See provides for his personal needs. If he needs Gummi bears for the nephews, Ray Bans, lift tickets or birthday cards, he can purchase them at whim. A member of his entourage will pick up the tab. Fortunately for the Vatican coffers, the Pope doesn't live in his own material world. Says the Vatican Embassy, he rarely has time for shopping.

Is what you forsee what you get?

For Pius XII it was. At his baptism, the priest held the infant Pius aloft and supposedly proclaimed, "In 63 years all of Rome and St. Peter's will be celebrating this man." And they did. On his 63rd birthday, just like the man said.

Prophesy footnote: As a young child, the future Pope Sixtus V (1585-90) was met on a street by the prophet Nostradamas, who knelt and said, "I must kneel before His Holiness." Nineteen years later, Sixtus was in the chair.

RESERVATIONS REQUIRED

ONLY MAJOR CREDIT CARDS ACCEPTED

Where do you learn to be a Pope?

 There is no Pope school to speak of, though there should be. Witness JPII. During his first days on the job, he would forget to give blessings at the end of audiences, and would wander into far-off Vatican offices, getting lost. The Vatican tailors were irked early on because he didn't have sleeves showing beneath his cassock. In truth, various Vatican staffers are charged with coaching fledgling Popes on papal protocol.

Q Is there a Vice Pope?

A Sort of, but not one that becomes Pope if the boss dies. The Vatican Second Banana is the Secretary of State, currently Cardinal Casaroli. When the Pope is on vacation, he keeps in close contact, but not, we hear, by beeper.

Who were the Papa Popes?

There have been plenty of Popes over the centuries who have fathered offspring, to wit, Alexander VI, father of Lucrezia Borgia (of poison fame), and Cesare, model for Machiavelli's "The Prince." But the real Papa Pope award would have to go to Pope Hormisdas (514-523) who fathered Pope Silverius (536-538). The word "pope," of course, means "father."

Does the Pope take dictation?

Only from the Man Upstairs. The Pope does type, though. Pius XII banged out his homilies and dissertations on a portable model, the first Pope to do so.

Can you depose a Pope?

Deposing Popes was all the rage in the old days. In just one example among many, The College of Cardinals, the electing body, couldn't decide who they wanted. They chose Urban VI, but five months later got tired of his tactlessness and brought Clement VII to replace him. But Urban wouldn't budge. So he stayed in Rome, Clement went off to Avignon, France, and they both spent the rest of their days excommunicating each other. It was finally decided that Urban was the real thing. Clement was declared an "anti-pope." But he excommunicated Urban anyway.

There have been those who have abdicated for better or worse; sometimes for love, other times for money, to say nothing of plain change of heart. Among the changelings Marcellinus (304), Liberius (366), Benedict IX (1044, '45 and '48), Gregory VI (1046), St. Celestine V (1294) and Gregory XII (1415).

These days, Popes don't usually leave their job unless the Boss calls.

Q Can the Pope hold a white-collar job?

A And we don't mean priestly collars, either. Plenty of pontiffs were professional as well as clerical. Innocent X (1644-55) was a judge, and Innocent XI (1676-89) a banker. Boniface VIII (1294-1303) was a lawyer; Eusebius (310) was a historian, as well as a doctor.

 What does the Pope do for Halloween?

 Trick-or-treaters aren't allowed inside the Vatican—boo!—but the Pope has been known to don a disguise or two. John XXIII (1958-63) dressed up as an anonymous priest during his nightly strolls. Nine hundred years earlier, Leo IX (1049-54) disguised himself as a pilgrim on his way to his Vatican coronation. The masses recognized him and cheered anyway, but they still didn't put candy in his sack.

Does the Pope send love letters?

John Paul I (1978) wrote rhapsodically of his affections —most notably, for Pinocchio the wooden puppet. But also for Shakespeare, the centuries-dead dramatist; and Figaro the opera hero. The love notes were published in JPI's "Illus-trimi," a compendium of his letters.

It is not known whether Pinocchio wrote back.

Q Who was that masked Pope? (Episode I)?

A After recovering from the attempt on his life in 1981, JPII slipped away to Portugal to pray before the Blessed Virgin Mary. He gave thanks for his survival. He left as his offering—you guessed it—a bullet, the one the surgeons removed from his body. No word on whether it was Heigh-Ho Silver.

Does the Pope go for light bedtime reading?

 When the current JP puts his PJs on, he likes to catch up on the newspapers, as did his predecessor, JPI. But Paul VI (1963-78) was a bit heavier. His servants carted 90 crates of books wherever he traveled. That way, Paul could satisfy his 1 a.m. craving for "Populorum Progressio," et al. Not the Reader's Digest version.

 Is the Pope an equal opportunity employer?

Let's just say he's come a long way since the Renaissance, when Pius V (1566-72), for one, confined Jews to ghettoes, accused them of witchcraft, forced them to wear identification badges, and excluded them from owning land. Not exactly enlightened.

Does the Pope do housework?

A Scrubbing windows is not in the Pope's job description. Butlers and maids do the holy housework. JPII even takes his help on the road. You can't expect a guy to serve communion wafers when he has dishpan hands.

Does the Pope have an investment portfolio?

He should. The Vatican may be rich, but its bank balance wasn't built in a day. It took more than 1,000 years to balance the books. Innocent XI (1676-89) was the first to do it, wiping away the debts of his predecessors. A few centuries of rosary beads later, in 1919 to be exact, the Vatican was rescued from bankruptcy again, this time by a loan from the Knights of Columbus. And after World War II, some papal funds were invested for safe keeping with the New York Stock Exchange. (Do insider trading laws apply to those with connections to the Ultimate Chairman of the Board?)

Can the Pope hold a bake sale?

Actually, the favorite papal fund raiser was selling indulgences. It was kind of an anti-bake sale: If you buy them, you won't bake. They guaranteed that the buyer was no longer responsible for a particular sin. Needless to say, they went like hotcakes. Or cupcakes. People hoarded them on "buy now, sin later" arrangements. Sixtus IV said in 1476 that indulgences also applied to souls in purgatory. Leo X (1513-21) came up with an eight-year sin-free special. Historians generally credit that line of thinking with the rise of Martin Luther and the Protestant Reformation. Some, no doubt full of sour grapes, say Luther simply couldn't make his payments.

Who was Sistine?

There was no Sistine. Sistine means "in the time of Sixtus," particularly Sixtus IV (1471-84), the same guy who said you could buy a ticket out of purgatory. He was a great patron of the arts, and is, in fact, credited with leading Rome into the Renaissance, chapel and all.

Did Pope Fabian sing?

Not that much is written about old Fab'—but we know that Gregory I (590-604), father of the chants, did. Leo II (682-83) was a choir school graduate known for his supple pipes. No record of whether he and Fabian toured together.

 Can a Pope go to war?

The Vatican's current stand is to sit them out. Not so during the Renaissance. Julius II (1503-13), the "Warrior Pope," thought nothing of suiting up in full armor and leading his crusaders into battle. He was known as "il terrible," at least behind his back. In a famous story, the artist Michelangelo was planning to place a book in the hands of a statue of Julius. The Pope told the artist no, put a sword there instead. But even with the sword the statue didn't survive.

Q Is there a minimum age for popehood?

A It might seem they're all graybeards, but in fact, papal lore has Benedict IX (1032-48) coming of age at 14. He is the one who abidcated in pursuit of marriage, returned a second time, and abidcated, and returned yet again. All before reaching 30.

John XII (955-64) was 17. Only a matter of time before the Hollywood version, "I Was a Teenage Pope."

Q Are diamonds a Pope's best friend?

A Popes have alway been fond of baubles, bangle and beads. JPII wears a wris watch (a Rolex?); Leo X (1513-21 decked his lovely long finger with jeweled rings. But the lord of papal rings had to be Juliu II (1503-13), of warrior fame, wh commissioned the papa jeweler to create the biggest gaudiest tiara in existence estimated cost: 10 millio francs. And that's in 151 money.

Can the Pope be a best seller?

 JPII, of course, is known for his stabs at poetry and plays. It seems he comes from a long line of papal literary luminaries. Pius II (1558-64) was a novelist and poet laureate. Among his works: an erotic comedy and his memoirs, not necessarily in that order.

Alexander VII (1655-67) was a famous poet. (Who can forget the immortal "Philmathi Musae inveniles"?)

Clement IX (1667-69) wrote poetry and religious dramas. He is also credited with taking comic opera seriously. The papal Gilbert and Sullivan?

Can you be a mail-order Pope?

 Paul VI (1963-78) was. He studied for the priesthood by correspondence courses. He came out of the closet after graduation to pursue further studies in Rome. He also saved a lot of money on stamps.

Who was that masked Pope? (Episode II)?

 That would be Leo X (1513-21). Notoriously homely—flabby, short, pock-marked, not your basic hunk—Leo was famous for hosting parties of all kinds, especially masked balls, popular even among the unmarked, in those days of yesteryear.

Q Does the Pope wear makeup?

A Leo X (1513-21) probably should have. He needed a good reason—like ratings. Pius XII (1939-58), the first Pope to appear on television, spruced himself up before air time with pancake.

Does the Pope order take-out?

Sure. He just takes it out of another country. Alexander VIII (1689-91) started the tradition of importing delicacies from France. John XXIII (1958-63) insisted that his Roquefort, Burgundy and bread be imported weekly. (John reportedly finished his papal acceptance speech with a resounding, "Now let's eat.") But papal feasting also has a flip side. Old Gregory (590-604) almost didn't make it to Greatness because of his rabid fasting. Not your midnight pizza monger.

What were Gregory's greatest hits?

 How about, "Hungry for Your Love," by rockin' Greg I, the faster.

"Eight (or More) Days a Week," by rollin' Gregory VII, (1073-85), who created the Gregorian Calendar.

"I Shot the Sheriff," by Gregory IX (1227-41), founder of the Spanish Inquisition.

Who made the Leonine Walls?

Leo IV (847-55) was the guy who built the wall around the Vatican to defend it from enemies. And you probably thought it was our boy Leo X (1513-21), hoping to keep out party crashers or mask pullers.

Q Can the Pope giveth and taketh away?

A Pius XI (1922-39) did. With one stroke of the pen he brought the Vatican up to modern standards by installing plumbing, elevators, a radio station and an all-electric kitchen. With another signature, he issued the famous Casti Connubii, the papal opinion rubber-stamping contraception as a mortal sin. Life in the kitchen hasn't been the same since.

How do you soothe an aching Pope?

Pius XII kept a bedside gramophone and listened to Wagner to ease his holy bones. JPII, aka the aerobi-pope, likes to swim to relax. We don't know if Popes ever called out for a massage.

 Can the Pope have a first lady?

We're not saying the bedside gramophone had anything to do with it, but according to some Vatican historians, Pius XII (1939-58) had a housekeeper/confidante/companion and unofficial mother hen, one Sister Pasqualina, head nun of the papal entourage. She hovered around him, telling Pi' when it was time to eat or go to bed, when he was standing in a draft, when someone was taking too much of his time, what to do with a particular gift. In short, she was the woman behind the man behind The Man.

Does the Pope give blood?

JPII does. To himself, at least. Before his 1987 trek to the United States, the pontiff stockpiled a whole body's worth of blood in case of emergency. He couldn't depend on local blood banks because of his rare blood type.

On less therapeutic fronts, plenty of early popes gave blood, but not voluntarily. The knock-'em-sock-'ems included John VIII (872-82), who was clubbed to death; Stephen VIII (939-42) who was imprisoned and mutilated; and Benedict V (964-66), whose papal sceptre was broken over his head. Lots of emergencies, but not too many emergency blood supplies.

Can the Pope filibuster?

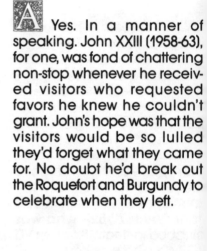 Yes. In a manner of speaking. John XXIII (1958-63), for one, was fond of chattering non-stop whenever he received visitors who requested favors he knew he couldn't grant. John's hope was that the visitors would be so lulled they'd forget what they came for. No doubt he'd break out the Roquefort and Burgundy to celebrate when they left.

Q Can the Pope start a fashion trend?

A John XXIII (1958-63) was probably the closet thing to a papal dandy. First, he commissioned a specially cobbled pair of red leather boots. Then he showed up wearing a red-felt cap with ermine ear muffs, a throwback to his 16th-century predecessors. Some say his sartorial savvy could have landed him in the fashionable men's mag, *GQ*. Or, is that *PQ*?

 Does the Pope gamble?

 Leo X was fond of throwing dice and betting on bullfights. But not so Benedict XIII (1724-30). He put an end to the public lottery, one of the Vatican's biggest money-makers. The lottery resumed in 1730, when Bennie's successor Clement XII was crowned. Clement was blinded two years after taking the papal throne, and spent most of his 10-year papacy bedridden with gout. That's not so lucky.

Can the Pope go bar-hopping?

Not if he stays at the Vatican. There's only one watering hole on the holy grounds.

 Does the Pope do commercials?

Leo XIII (1878-1903) wrote a testimonial for a French chemist who created a cocaine-laced wine cooler called Vin Mariani. The label called the product an "unequaled tonic-stimulant for fatigued or overworked body or brain." Perfect for a pooped Pope.

Does the Pope talk in his sleep?

John XXIII (1958-63) was just as much a chatterer in sleep as in wake. Some sources recall the pontiff mulling over problems in his dreams, mumbling "I'll have to ask the Pope," before surfacing to consciousness and realizing, "But I am the Pope." It still didn't solve his problems.

Can the Pope go Hollywood?

 JPII did. On his 1987 arrival in Southern California, he found that someone had altered the famous Hollywood sign to read "Holywood." No one to date has claimed responsibility. Some suspect Divine Intervention. JPII didn't take offense, but he didn't check out the Sunset Strip, either.

Does the Pope like penguins?

We're not sure where the Church is on this, but we do know that JPII, in his exhaustive travels, has visited 67 countries and every continent except Antarctica. The pontiff may wear an occasional sport shirt with penguin over pocket, but the real birds are still waiting for their blessing. Maybe that's why they can't fly.

Suppose they gave a papal funeral and nobody came?

 That happened to Sabinian (604-06), successor of Gregory the Great (590-604), admittedly a tough act to follow. Sabinian wasn't popular. For one thing, he got rich from selling grain during a famine. When Sabinian died, his funeral procession had to detour to be kept away from the angry throngs. His burial place was kept secret so the mob wouldn't steal his body. They didn't make it to the wake, either.

When was the Pope first a Pope

Some scholars say Callistus I (217-22) was the first to be called Pope, for papa, or father. Until that time, head honchos were called "Episcopus," which basically means "Big Guy Bishop." Callistus was a former convict who worked the salt mines of Sardinia. Among his crimes was brawling in a synagogue during the Sabbath. The original Big Daddy!

Is being Pope a family affair?

John Paul II is an orphan Pope. His mother and brother died when he was a child, and his father, when he was a college student. But there are papal families. If you really want to talk papal family ties, you'd have to go back to Greg I, whose noble family produced three popes: Felix III (483-92), who scholars believe is great-grandfather of the Great Guy; Greg, and Agapitus I (535-36), for whom some say the name "pope" was first used. But when you go back that far, nothing is certain. Just ask Daddy-O Callistus.

How many Popes does it take to screw in a light bulb?

In the convoluted workings of papal history, that's not easy to answer, but in the case of Leo XII (1823-29), it would have to be none. A backward looker, Leo banned Vatican gaslights and other modern amenities. He is blamed for returning the Vatican to the Dark Ages.

Fortunately, his successor, Pius VIII (1829-30), shed new light on Vatican modernism. He took the name of the forward-looking Pope Pius VII (1800-23), Leo's predecessor, and let there be light again.

Does the Pope play marbles?

 Benedict XV (1914-22) didn't. He played priest with the toy altar his grandmother had given him.

His close relationship with his grandmother may account for this Pope's feminism. He canonized Joan of Arc.

Some people thought he'd lost his marbles.

Name	Reigned From	To
St. Peter	-	67
St. Linus	67	76
St. Anacletus (Cletus)	76	88
St. Clement	88	97
St. Evaristus	97	105
St. Alexander I	105	115
St. Sixtus I	115	125
St. Telesphorus	125	136
St. Hyginus	136	140
St. Pius I	140	155
St. Anicetus	155	166
St. Soter	166	175
St. Eleutherius	175	189
St. Victor I	189	199
St. Zephyrinus	199	217
St. Callistus I	217	222
St. Urban I	222	230
St. Pontian	230	235
St. Anterus	235	236
St. Fabian	236	250
St. Cornelius	251	253
St. Lucius I	253	254
St. Stephen I	254	257
St. Sixtus II	257	258
St. Dionysius	259	268
St. Felix I	269	274
St. Eutychian	275	283
St. Caius	283	296
St. Marcellinus	296	304
St. Marcellus I	308	309
St. Eusebius	309	309
St. Meltiades	311	314
St. Sylvester I	314	335

Name	Reigned From	To
St. Marcus	336	336
St. Julius I	337	352
Liberius	352	366
St. Damasus I	366	384
St. Siricius	384	399
St. Anastasius I	399	401
St. Innocent I	401	417
St. Zozimus	417	418
St. Boniface I	418	422
St. Celestine I	422	432
St. Sixtus III	432	440
St. Leo I (the Great)	440	461
St. Hilary	461	468
St. Simplicius	468	483
St. Felix III (II)	483	492
St. Gelasius I	492	496
Anastasius II	496	498
St. Symmachus	498	514
St. Hormisdas	514	523
St. John I	523	526
St. Felix IV (III)	526	530
Boniface II	530	532
John II	533	535
St. Agapitus I	535	536
St. Silverius	536	537
Vigilius	537	555
Pelagius I	556	561
John III	561	574
Benedict I	575	579
Pelagius II	579	590
St. Gregory I (the Great)	590	604
Sabinianus	604	606

Name	Reigned From	To	Name	Reigned From	To
Boniface III	607	607	Eugene II	824	827
St. Boniface IV	608	615	Valentine	827	827
St. Deusdedit (Adeodatus I)	615	618	Gregory IV	827	844
			Sergius II	844	847
Boniface V	619	625	St. Leo IV	847	855
Honorius I	625	638	Benedict III	855	858
Severinus	640	640	St. Nicholas I (the Great)	858	867
John IV	640	642			
Theodore I	642	649	Adrian II	867	872
St. Martin I	649	655	John VIII	872	882
St. Eugene I	654	657	Marinus I	882	884
St. Vitalian	657	672	St. Adrian III	884	885
Adeodatus II	672	676	Stephen V (VI)	885	891
Donus	676	678	Formosus	891	896
St. Agatho	678	681	Boniface VI	896	896
St. Leo II	682	683	Stephen VI (VII)	896	897
St. Benedict II	684	685	Romanus	897	897
John V	685	686	Theodore II	897	897
Conon	686	687	John IX	898	900
St. Sergius I	687	701	Benedict IV	900	903
John VI	701	705	Leo V	903	903
John VII	705	707	Sergius III	904	911
Sisinnius	708	708	Anastasius III	911	913
Constantine	708	715	Landus	913	914
St. Gregory II	715	731	John X	914	928
St. Gregory III	731	741	Leo VI	928	928
St. Zachary	741	752	Stephen VII (VIII)	928	931
Stephen II (III)	752	757	John XI	931	935
St. Paul I	757	767	Leo VII	936	939
Stephen III (IV)	768	772	Stephen VIII (IX)	939	942
Adrian I	772	795	Marinus II	942	946
St. Leo III	795	816	Agapitus II	946	955
Stephen IV (V)	816	817	John XII	955	963
St. Paschal I	817	824	Leo VIII	963	964

Name	Reigned From	To	Name	Reigned From	To
Benedict V	964	965	Innocent II	1130	1143
John XIII	965	972	Celestine II	1143	1144
Benedict VI	973	974	Lucius II	1144	1145
Benedict VII	974	983	Bl. Eugene III	1145	1153
John XIV	983	984	Anastasius IV	1153	1154
John XV	985	996	Adrian IV	1154	1159
Gregory V	996	999	Alexander III	1159	1181
Sylvester II	999	1003	Lucius III	1181	1185
John XVII	1003	1003	Urban III	1185	1187
John XVIII	1004	1009	Gregory VIII	1187	1187
Sergius IV	1009	1012	Clement III	1187	1191
Benedict VIII	1012	1024	Celestine III	1191	1198
John XIX	1024	1032	Innocent III	1198	1216
Benedict IX	1032	1044	Honorius III	1216	1227
Sylvester III	1045	1045	Gregory IX	1227	1241
Benedict IX (2nd time)	1045	1045	Celestine IV	1241	1241
			Innocent IV	1243	1254
Gregory VI	1045	1046	Alexander IV	1254	1261
Clement II	1046	1047	Urban IV	1261	1264
Benedict IX (3rd time)	1047	1048	Clement IV	1265	1268
			Bl. Gregory X	1271	1276
Damasus II	1048	1048	Bl. Innocent V	1276	1276
St. Leo IX	1049	1054	Adrian V	1276	1276
Victor II	1055	1057	John XXI	1276	1277
Stephen IX (X)	1057	1058	Nicholas III	1277	1280
Nicholas II	1059	1061	Martin IV	1281	1285
Alexander II	1061	1073	Honorius IV	1285	1287
St. Gregory VII	1073	1085	Nicholas IV	1288	1292
Bl. Victor III	1086	1087	St. Celestine V	1294	1294
Bl. Urban II	1088	1099	Boniface VIII	1294	1303
Paschal II	1099	1118	Bl. Benedict XI	1303	1304
Gelasius II	1118	1119	Clement V	1305	1314
Callistus II	1119	1124	John XXII	1316	1334
Honorius II	1124	1130	Benedict XII	1334	1342

Name	Reigned From	To	Name	Reigned From	To
Clement VI	1342	1352	Leo XI	1605	1605
Innocent VI	1352	1362	Paul V	1605	1621
Bl. Urban V	1362	1370	Gregory XV	1621	1623
Gregory XI	1370	1378	Urban VIII	1623	1644
Urban VI	1378	1389	Innocent X	1644	1655
Boniface IX	1389	1404	Alexander VII	1655	1667
Innocent VII	1404	1406	Clement IX	1667	1669
Gregory XII	1406	1415	Clement X	1670	1676
Martin V	1417	1431	Bl. Innocent XI	1676	1689
Eugene IV	1431	1447	Alexander VIII	1689	1691
Nicholas V	1447	1455	Innocent XII	1691	1700
Callistus III	1455	1458	Clement XI	1700	1721
Pius II	1458	1464	Innocent XIII	1721	1724
Paul II	1464	1471	Benedict XIII	1724	1730
Sixtus IV	1471	1484	Clement XII	1730	1740
Innocent VIII	1484	1492	Benedict XIV	1740	1758
Alexander VI	1492	1503	Clement XIII	1758	1769
Pius III	1503	1503	Clement XIV	1769	1774
Julius II	1503	1513	Pius VI	1775	1799
Leo X	1513	1521	Pius VII	1800	1823
Adrian VI	1522	1523	Leo XII	1823	1829
Clement VII	1523	1534	Pius VIII	1829	1830
Paul III	1534	1549	Gregory XVI	1831	1846
Julius III	1550	1555	Pius IX	1846	1878
Marcellus II	1555	1555	Leo XIII	1878	1903
Paul IV	1555	1559	St. Pius X	1903	1914
Pius IV	1559	1565	Benedict XV	1914	1922
St. Pius V	1566	1572	Pius XI	1922	1939
Gregory XIII	1572	1585	Pius XII	1939	1958
Sixtus V	1585	1590	John XXIII	1958	1963
Urban VII	1590	1590	Paul VI	1963	1978
Gregory XIV	1590	1591	John Paul I	1978	1978
Innocent IX	1591	1591	John Paul II	1978	
Clement VIII	1592	1605			

BIBLIOGRAPHY

Aradi, Zsolt; "The Popes: The History of How They Are Chosen, Elected and Crowned," Farrar, Strauss and Cudahy, 1955.

Balsoni, Carlo; "The Silence of Pius XII," Little, Brown and Co., 1965.

Barraclough, Geoffrey; "The Medieval Papacy," Thames and Hudson, 1968.

Chadwick, Owedn; "The Reformation," a Pelican history of the Church.

Chamberlain, E.R.; "The Bad Popes," Dial Press, 1969.

Cheetham, Nicholas; "Keepers of the Keys," Scribners, 1983.

Durant, Will and Ariel; "The Story of Civilization, Vol. VIII: The Age of Louis XIV," Simon and Schuster, 1963.

Fesquet, Henri; "Wit and Wisdom of Good Pope John," PJ Kenedy & Sons, 1964.

Fraser, Antonia; "Cromwell The Lord Protector," Alfred A. Knopf, 1973.

Gontard, Friedrich; "The Popes," Barrie and Rockliff.

Greystone; "The Popes: A Concise Biographical History Vol. I and II," Hawthorne Books, 1964.

Henze, Anton; "The Pope and the World," Viking Press, 1965

Hebbiethwaite, Peter, and Kaufman, Ludwig; "John Paul II: A Pictorial Biography," McGraw-Hill Book Co., 1979.

Kelly, J.N.D., "The Oxford Dictionary of Popes," Oxford, 1986.

Kiefer, S.M., Brother William; "Leo XIII: A Light From Heaven," Bruce Publishing Co.

Malinski, Mieczysian; "Pope John Paul II: The Life of Karol Wojtyla," Seabury Press, 1979.

Neville, Robert; "The World of the Vatican," Harper and Row, 1962.

Nichols, Peter; "The Pope's Divisions: The Roman Catholic Church Today," Holt, Rinehart and Winston, 1981.

L'Osservatore Romano newspaper, Vatican City 1987 issues

Sugrue, Francis; "Popes in the Modern World," Thomas Y. Crowell Co., 1961.

Thomas, Gordon; "Desire and Denial," Little Brown and Co., 1986.

Tuchman, Barbara W.; "The March of Folly," Alfred A. Knopf, 1984.

Walsh, Michael; "An Illustrated History of the Popes: St. Peter to John Paul II."